To Bob,
Port... it's
not just for
drinking anymore!
Cheers,
Holly

PORT

{the secret ingredient}

Creatively Cooking with Port Wine

PORT

{the secret ingredient}

Creatively Cooking with Port Wine

by Holly Meyer

{& Friends}

Dedication

To my partners at Meyer Family Port
and to all of the port drinkers and foodies
the world over!

Printed in U.S.A. by Signature Book Printing, www.sbpbooks.com

Food and Prop Styling by HOLLY MEYER
Designed by HOLLY MEYER
  Graphic Design Consultant, Shirin Ardakani, I Heart CMYK
Typesetting by HOLLY MEYER
Distributed by DBA Port, The Secret Ingredient

Rating System for the Port Recipes

I have categorized the recipes with a wine glass logo that indicates the intensity of the Port flavor you can expect in each dish. The rating starts with one glass, meaning the dish has just a suggestion or whiff of Port, all the way up to five glasses, giving you fair warning that the Port is at it's fullest flavor and just might deliciously overwhelm your taste buds.

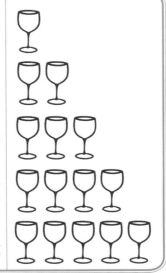

A Wiff of Port

A Sip of Port

A Glass of Port

Just a bit Tipsy
(maybe 1 glass more)

Complete Seduction
(Enjoy the whole bottle! You know you want to!)

Contents

It takes a village to do anything right, and that is especially true of this book. Without the support, guidance and occasional harassment from my close friends and family, it would not have come together. In my mind, I feel as though this book has many authors, many wise elders. While it would take another book to thank everyone for their contributions, there are certain people that I must acknowledge here by name.

Acknowledgements

Thank You to all of my faithful and wonderful testers and eaters. Thank you to the many, many people whose ideas, suggestions, knowledge, and comments helped me arrive at the final selection of recipes, among them Shirin, Becky, Desiree, Candice, Kelsey, Darcy, Mike, Sheila, Conrad, Matt, Jerry, Cindy, Daniel, Evelyn, Ruggero, Paula, Shawn, Pat, Victor, Narisa, Trihn, Ceila, Norma, Josh, and Teri. I would like to give a special thank you to Meyer Family Cellars for supplying the exceptional Port that we used in all of the recipe testing. I am thankful to Teri Flynn for the title, Port: The Secret Ingredient. And as always, thank you to my mother, Bonny, for her support, encouragement, help in the kitchen and for being the dishwasher without complaint.

Introduction

I am a child of the Napa Valley, and when I was born, wine enthusiasts already knew about the vineyards covering our gently rolling hills and our wines that rivaled those of Europe. However, as I grew up, the Napa Valley witnessed an explosion of artisanal farms and outstanding restaurants, an influx of innovative chefs transforming this abundance into exciting new dishes that complimented California wines. Eventually, I became a partner in our family's wine business. By that time, Meyer Family Port had already made a name for itself among connoisseurs of fine dessert wines. But something nagged at me. Something was missing from the traditional marriage of fine wine and great food. I was shocked at how few people knew about the virtues of Port as more than just an after dinner drink. Why weren't the gifted chefs around me using Port to enhance their dishes, to deepen and enrich the flavors of the bounty they used in their kitchens? I made the radical decision to fill this gap and take on the task of writing, compiling, brainstorming, sharing, cooking and tasting recipes that incorporate and compliment Port.

As my idea to write a Port cookbook took shape, I organized tasting parties and sent out a call to my family and friends to try out some dishes. "Come on over," I'd say. "Bring your dishes with Port and ideas for dishes with Port. Get ready to brainstorm names for the book and recipes." We gathered once a month for four straight months. We cooked, ate, drank, and laughed over some of the initial bad titles for the book (including some awful puns). We rated all the dishes and reworked anything we didn't think was exceptional.

In the end, with the help of my friends and family, I was able to combine my love of Port and passion for cooking (that I believe we share or else you wouldn't have picked up this book) into a unique collection of dishes that I hope will enlighten the world about the incredible dynamic flavors and versatility of Port. All of the recipes that made the final cut received rave reviews. I hope you'll agree.

A Very Brief History of Port

Port has a complicated history and it's hard to pin down the accuracy of all the stories swirling around this legendary wine. When war broke out between England and France in the 1680's England could no longer obtain French wines and turned to Portugal to quench its thirst. However, Portuguese grown grapes in the Duoro region at the time were considered extremely harsh and of poor quality. How this inferior wine turned into an extraordinary blend is actually still a mystery, however, here are a couple of intriguing theories.

Theory #1: Some say that the wine demand was so high that the Portuguese developed the strategy of shipping barrels of mature, but young, wine before the aging process was complete, so that the wine didn't waste time in the wineries or on the docks. On route, the sailors would add brandy to stabilize the young wine to decrease the chance of shock to the wine during the long journey to England. This process sped up the maturing process of the wine and they began dousing the wine with brandy earlier and earlier until they were introducing it into the fermentation process. Ta-dah! They had created Port.

Theory #2: The English actually had the idea of fortifying inferior wine, although they usually used whisky. This idea killed to birds with one stone as it would make a higher alcohol content and make an inferior wine tolerable. The English introduced this idea to the Portuguese sailors and from there Theory #1 evolved. And Portugal has taken the credit for it? Scandalous!

Theory #3: Merchants from Liverpool searched for a wine source in Portugal's Duoro Valley. There they stumbled across an abbot in a monastery in Lamego who was adding brandy during the fermentation process in order to increase the alcoholic content. Cheeky fellow! The merchants realized that this wine that the abbot was making made a concentrate of some sort. By adding the brandy to the wine higher alcohol content was made with little effort, so that once the Port arrived on English shores, the merchants could add water to mixture and get twice as much product for their buck.

Whichever way you spill the story, someone discovered the magnificent idea of adding Brandy during the fermentation process, thus stopping the development of the wine, keeping it sweet, fruity and strong (due to the added brandy, of course). Fortunately for England, this improved the harsh wine from Portugal and the low price (due to large quantities, or watered down supplies) inevitably made it extremely popular. Fortunately for wine lovers, a new varietal was born and Port evolved into a full-bodied and enjoyable after-dinner delicacy.

Meyer Family Port, a History

While this is not a book merely to extol Meyer Family Port, I'd like to explain how my interest in Port began. My father, Justin Meyer, started making Port and other fortified wines in the 1960's when he was a member of the Christian Brothers Catholic order in Napa Valley. I know what you are thinking, and yes, my father was a monk, but that is a whole other story. The important fact, and especially most crucial to my personal existence, was that my father left the order for my mother and started to make wine in the Napa Valley.

Rather than regale you with my interpretation of how we all started-- I was 10 when I realized that we even made Port and my details are a bit fuzzy and inaccurate--I am going give you the story the more accurate historian in the family tells, my mother, Bonny Meyer (which is a funny coincidence since I technically am a historian by trade, but we won't go into that). She was there early on and knows the stories told by close family friends who knew my father back during his Christian Brother days.

"It all started over a Pinochle game held every Tuesday night up in the Brother's "Family Room," she likes to say. Christian Brothers Justin, Tom, Luke, Greg, and sometimes Fred would gather for the standing card game around 7pm and would play for nickels and dimes till 1 or 2 in the morning. "You see," she explains, "they didn't have to get up for early Mass on Wednesday mornings, so they would stay up

WARNING: *Meyer Family Port was exclusively used in the writing and the enjoying of all recipes. The subtle raspberry and light sweetness of this 10-year tawny Port is a vital contribution to the amount of sugar and the kinds of ingredients added to recipes. USE of other Ports is at your own Risk!*

half the night playing cards and drinking pot still Brandy (type of process for making Brandy) and Tawny and Ruby Port."

It didn't take too long for young Brother Justin (later to become my father) to develop an appreciation for Port. In training at Christian Brothers Winery under legendary cellarmaster, Brother Timothy, Justin quickly picked up the ability to taste a wine's architecture and perceive subtle varietal nuances. After a long day in the cellar or vineyard, he appreciated a great glass of Port and a good cigar as much as anybody.

After many years as a Christian Brother, Justin left the monastery and founded Silver Oak, producer of world-class Cabernet Sauvignon. But he never forgot those crazy card games or lost his love of Port. So years later, when the Christian Brothers decided to stop making Port, he started. He bought a couve' of Touriga Nacional (a varietal of grape), put it in some oak barrels, and Meyer Family Port was born.

My mother concludes her story with a touch of bragging (as any mother would) by saying, "Today, son, Matt, makes our Port with the same appreciation and dedication to producing a great end-of-the-day experience. Now daughter, Holly, has taken the appreciation of Port a few steps further by bringing you over 60 ways to cook with and enjoy this great classic wine. So if, after eating some Beef Tenderloin with Port Sauce or finishing your meal with Holly's divine Meyer Family Port Chocolate Truffles, you feel like playing a little cards, know you are tapping into the spirit of those long ago evenings up in the Christian Brothers monastery at Mont La Salle. Play for nickels and dimes, drink some Port, tell jokes and laugh a lot."

Meyer Family Port, Tasting Notes
by Tony Poer, Meyer Family Port Sales Manager

"Meyer Family Port, the fortified Zinfandel made by Matt and Karen Meyer at their winery in Mendocino County, occupies a unique position on the surprisingly long list of sweet wines produced in California. Most of these wines are made for tasting room crowds or mailing lists, or otherwise fall into the "afterthought dessert wine" category. The Meyers' Port, on the other hand, is an unfailing show-stopper.

NOTE: *The wine tasting notes, complimenting notes, chef's notes and suggestions are all optional, but strongly recommended.*

During the past several years that I've worked as the winery's sales manager, it's given me great pleasure to present the wine to a wide variety of retail and restaurant establishments. The reactions to the Port have been almost uniformly positive—and often ecstatic—with even the most jaded of sommeliers or retailers taking note of its rich, complex, and balanced flavors. It has even found a niche among mixologists in the cutting-edge San Francisco cocktail culture. By nature a "sweet" wine, the Port falls automatically into the dessert category, but the wine is so much more interesting for its balancing acidity, its spicy-nutty undertones, and, perhaps most importantly, its amazing food compatibility. It pairs seamlessly with an elaborate, savory course, such as a blue cheese soufflé, and yet a relatively humble dessert like apple pie is also a fine complement. Indeed, apples and cherries are among the foods that bring out the fortified Zinfandel's more subtle fruit flavors. The Port is well-accompanied during a cheese course by roasted nuts and any number of fine blue cheeses, English farmhouse Stilton being perhaps the ideal choice. And dark chocolate desserts are, of course, the default pairing for this extraordinary fortified wine."

Tips for Cooking with Port

Port is a strong, full, well-rounded, but rich dessert wine. An easy route to go with this information is to pair it with full-bodied dishes served in winter. An obvious dessert choice with a Red Zinfandel tawny Port? Death by chocolate, of course. Yes, this Port cookbook contains pairings of foods commonly served with Port. However, the recipes that were the most fun to create were light dishes that contrasted with every flavor present in the Port. We also experimented with recipes not typically

WARNING: *When making Port sauces or reductions in an uncovered saucepan over heat, beware that alcohol does burn off into the air. You will become drunk on the fumes if you don't have a fan or meter your H2O intake. You will have a pretty heavy hangover if you don't. Trust me, I speak from experience!*

matched with Port. For example, my dear friends who are co-creators and hosts of our local monthly dinner party suggested brunch menus. Who drinks and cooks with Port for breakfast/brunch? That's right! We do! Why not? And I must say, it is my favorite section of the book. Those dishes offered some of our biggest culinary challenges, but it produced some of the most satisfying recipes. (Seriously, try the bacon recipe, if you don't believe me!?)

Writing this cookbook also helped me discover new means of enjoying Port. I

TASTING NOTES: *Made in a modified solera method, Meyer Family Port is one of California's signature fortified wines. This rich and complex Port is a blend of several vintages of old-vine Zinfandel that average eight years of age at release. On the nose, Meyer Family Port displays aromas of baked fruit and cooking spice, along with warm notes of alembic Zinfandel brandy. Rich and round on the palate, its lush flavors of sweet cassis and brandied cherries are framed by integrated oak and fine acidity.*

had asked my brother Matthew, co-owner and co-winemaker of Meyer Family Cellars, for any suggestions on recipes to add to the cookbook. What he had to say totally surprised me! His suggestion, and one of his personal favorites, was to compliment Port with a citrus dish or dessert. The normal tendency is to compliment a sweet Port with a sweet and heavy chocolaty dessert. He said, "Instead of overpowering a subtle Port with a heavy dessert, why not contrast it with an acidic flavor that will really set off the complexities of the Port." So, at one of our tasting parties, we had Meyer Lemon Ice Cream and a lemon cake with lavender whip cream, and it was an unmitigated success for how it went with a glass of Port. The lemon contrast was a huge hit! I would not have guessed to pair lemon with Port. Another imaginative suggestion from Matt was Grilled Peaches with Sweet Port Sauce, a simple recipe that calls for tossing summer ripe peaches in olive oil, placing them on the grill and the drizzling them with Port. In this cookbook, I have just scratched the surface of Port pairing possibilities. Have fun with it, and if you come up with any new and interesting Port recipes, be sure to let me know!

Rating System for the Port Recipes

I have categorized the recipes with a wine glass logo that indicates the intensity of the Port flavor you can expect in each dish. The rating starts with one glass, meaning the dish has just a suggestion or whiff of Port, all the way up to five glasses, giving you fair warning that the Port is at it's fullest flavor and just might deliciously overwhelm your taste buds.

A Wiff of Port

A Sip of Port

A Glass of Port

Just a bit Tipsy
(maybe 1 glass more)

Complete Seduction
(Enjoy the whole bottle!
You know you want to!)

{I} Port & Chocolate

Meyer Family Port Chocolate Truffles
Raspberry Port Brownies
Chocolate Port Sauce
Candi's Chocolate Chip Cookies and Port Drizzle
Candi Cake's Frosting

*The first Meyer Family Port recipe,
also known as, the rich chocolaty
recipe that started it all!*

Meyer Family Port Chocolate Truffles

Makes (12) 1 ounces. Truffles
Ganache
8 ounces bittersweet chocolate,
finely chopped
3 tablespoons Meyer Family Port
1 tablespoons raspberry puree
4 tablespoons unsalted butter
4 tablespoons heavy whipping cream

Coating
Roll in ground chocolate
OR
8 ounces bittersweet chocolate
4 teaspoons canola oil
2 ounces white chocolate

Ganache
Place 8 ounces chocolate in a large stainless steel bowl and set aside. Place butter and cream in a pot over medium heat and bring to a simmer. Pour butter and cream mixture over chocolate. Let stand for 1 minute. Incorporate the butter and cream mixture into the chocolate using a wire whisk. Start mixing in the center of the bowl with small circles and gradually incorporate more chocolate by making larger circles until smooth. Add and stir in Meyer Family Port and Raspberry Puree to chocolate mixture. Pour into a shallow container and chill until firm for approximately 4 hours. (The depth of the chocolate will determine how long it takes for the mixture to set.)

When chocolate filling is set, shape by hand or use miniature ice cream scoop, place on a parchment lined sheet pan, refrigerate until ready to dip.

Coating
Melt bittersweet chocolate in a double boiler. (Not to exceed 115 degrees F) Remove from heat and add and whisk in oil. (Perfect dipping temperature is between 85-90 degrees F). Drop truffles into melted dipping chocolate and remove with a chocolate fork and place on parchment paper to harden.

Melt white chocolate in a double boiler. Once melted, remove from heat and drizzle in desired pattern.

Raspberry Port Brownies
Inspired by a friend

Makes 16 Brownies
(or 32 small bite size brownies)
3/4 cup butter (1-1/2 sticks)
4 ounces dark chocolate, finely chopped
3 eggs
1-1/2 cups sugar
1/4 cup raspberry puree
1/3 cup of Meyer Family Port
1 cup flour
1/4 teaspoon salt
1 cup chocolate chips (or dark chocolate, coarsely chopped)

Set oven to bake and preheat to 350°F. Grease 8" square pan, flour greased pan to limit batter from sticking.

Melt butter and chocolate over medium heat in medium saucepan. Remove from heat when melted.

In medium sized bowl, whisk together eggs, sugar, raspberry puree and port. Add melted butter and chocolate and whisk together.

Combine flour, salt and chocolate chips into small bowl and stir together. Add to wet ingredients and stir in. Transfer batter to greased and floured 8"x8" pan.

Bake at 350°F for 1 hour and 15 minutes or until knife comes out smooth.

Ahhhh... The Raspberry Port Brownie Recipe! Tasty and Luxurious! It is quite sinful!

Chocolate Port Sauce

Makes 2 cups
3/4 cup whipping cream
1/4 cup whole milk
1/4 cup unsalted butter (1/2 stick)
8 ounces dark chocolate, finely chopped
1/3 cup of Meyer Family Port

Place chocolate in a medium bowl and set aside.

Bring whipping cream, whole milk, and unsalted butter to simmer in small heavy saucepan. Pour over chocolate and let it sit for a minute. Whisk mixture until smooth. Stir in port and enjoy.

Chef's Notes
* Can be made 2 days ahead of time. Cover and chill and rewarm over medium-low heat.

Candi's Chocolate Chip Cookies with Port Drizzle

From the Kitchen of Candice Buckett

Makes 4 douncesen

Cookies

3 cup Flour
1 cup unsalted soften butter
1 cup granulated sugar
1 cup brown sugar
1 teaspoon vanilla
1 teaspoon baking soda
1/2 teaspoon salt
2 eggs
12 ounces of milk or dark chocolate chips

Chocolate Sauce

2 tablespoon milk
2 tablespoon butter
1 cup milk or dark chocolate chips
3 tablespoon of Meyer Family Port

Cookies

Preheat oven to 375°F

In a large bowl with an electric mixer blend together flour, sugars, soda and salt at a low speed.

Add butter and vanilla to mix, scrape down sides of the bowl to blend well. Add eggs and blend on medium speed for about 1 minute. Blend in chocolate chips to mix.

Place tablespoon rounds on to lightly greased cookie sheet about 2" apart. Bake for about 10-12 minutes or until golden brown. Transfer cookies immediately to parchment paper to cool.

Chocolate Sauce

Melt butter with milk on low in a small sauce pan. Fold in chocolate chips, once melted stir in port. Drizzle over cookies, or dip in one side.

Candi Cake's Frosting
From the Kitchen of Candice Buckett

Makes 12 Servings
3 cups confectioners sugar
6 tablespoons dark chocolate
cocoa powder
6 tablespoons soften
unsalted butter
5 tablespoons Meyer
Family Port
1 teaspoon vanilla extract

In a medium bowl, blend sugar and cocoa powder.

In a large bowl, cream butter until smooth, then beat in sugar mixture. Blend in vanilla and port, beat until light and fluffy. Frost cooled cupcakes.

"Enjoy this frosting on your favorite type of cupcake."
- Candice Buckett

{II} Beverages

Sangria

Rosy Cheek Fizz

Port Raspberry Lemonade

Glühwein

Welcome in the Summer with a glass.... or a pitcher of Sangria.

Sangria

Makes about 30 Servings
(6) 500 ml bottles of Meyer
Family Port
1/2 cup Cointreau
1 quart orange juice
1 cup lemon juice
2 oranges, thinly sliced
1 lemon, thinly sliced
2 Fuji apples, cored and chopped
(or 1 apple & 1 pear)
1 quart chilled club soda

Pour the half of the port, Cointreau, orange juice, and lemon juice into a large punch bowl. Add fresh cut fruit to the bowl. Add the remaining port and club soda to the bowl. Place bowl in refrigerator and chill for 3 to 24 hours.

Rosy Cheek Fizz
From the Bar of Daniel Hyatt, Mixologist

Makes 1 Serving
1 ounce Sloe Gin
1 ounce of Meyer Family Port
1/2 ounce lemon juice
2 teaspoon powdered Sugar
1 dash orange bitters
1 egg white
Sparkling wine (Suggestion: Cava)
1 drop rose water

Put first 6 ingredients in a shaker and shake without ice for a few seconds to foam the egg, add 3 or 4 large ice cubes and shake again vigorously for 20 seconds. Strain into a chilled highball glass and top with sparkling wine. Finish with a drop of rose water and a single rose petal.

This recipe can also be scaled up and served as a punch, in which case you would want to whip up the egg whites separately until soft peaks start to form. Mix sloe gin, port, lemon, powdered sugar and bitters in a punch bowl until sugar dissolved, stir in egg whites and then add sparkling wine. Garnish with rose petals, raspberries and slices of lemon and orange. Even pomegranate seed would be a fun addition to the punch.

Raspberry Port Lemonade
Inspired by a friend

Makes about 1 Quart
10 raspberries
2 ounces of Meyer Family Port
3/4 ounce vodka
3/4 ounce lemon juice
1/4 cup club soda
1/4 ounce sugar syrup (optional)
1/2 egg white
Ice cubes
Lime Wedge

Blend all ingredients without ice, strain into a highball glass filled with ice and garnish with a lime wedge.

Glühwein

Makes 8 Servings
1-1/2 cups of water
2 cinnamon sticks, broken into
1 to 2 inch pieces
1 teaspoon (heaped) of mixed
ground spices – allspice, nutmeg &
coriander together
1 orange
16 whole cloves
750 ml (1-1/2 bottles) of Meyer
Family Port

Put water in large saucepan and place over medium heat. Add cinnamon and spices.

Cut the orange into quarter lengthways, then cut them in half so you have eight pieces. Push two of the cloves into the skin of each piece and add to the pan. Pour in the port. Bring the heat up. It should not boil, so when bubbles start rising, turn the heat off. Taste for sweetness. If it is not sweet enough add sugar to taste and stir to dissolve.

Cover and let pan stand for an hour or longer so the flavors develop. Warm gently and strain before serving and serve in heat proof glass. Optionally garnish with a fresh stick of cinnamon.

A modification to the classic Austrian way to warm up in a Blustery Winter's Day or Night. It is classically offered at the Christmas Markets in Europe.

{III} Breakfast

Port French Toast

Mixed Berry Compote

Port Caramelized Bacon

Portified Waffles & Pancakes

Desi's Drunken Raspberry Crumb Cake

Mushroom and Gruyere Bread Pudding

Port French Toast
Inspired by a friend

Makes 4 Servings
6 tablespoons unsalted butter
6 tablespoons (packed) golden brown sugar
1-1/2 cups whole milk
3 large eggs
1/2 cup of Meyer Family Port
1-1/2 teaspoons ground cinnamon
1/2 teaspoon ground nutmeg
8 (1-inch) thick slices French bread

Pure maple syrup
& Berry Compote or
fresh blueberries and raspberries

Mix room temperature butter and brown sugar in small bowl to blend. Whisk milk, eggs, port, and spices in large bowl to blend. Melt 2 tablespoons brown sugar-butter mixture in large nonstick skillets over medium-high heat. Dip bread slices 1 at a time in egg mixture to coat. Add 4 slices to skillet. Cook until bottoms are deep brown, 3 to 4 minutes. Spread some of the butter mixture over the bread in the skillet. Turn slices over. Cook until bottoms are deep brown, 3 to 4 minutes. Cook second batch. (Or cook both batches simultaneously in 2 skillets)

(Optional and to taste) Sift powdered sugar over French toast. Top with berry compote or fresh berries. Drizzle with maple syrup.

Mixed Berry Compote

Makes about 2 Cups
3 tablespoons unsalted butter
1/4 cup packed light brown sugar
1-1/2 cup of Meyer Family Port
3 cups mixed berries (3/4 pound)
such as raspberries, blackberries,
and blueberries
1 (3-inch) cinnamon stick
2 fresh thyme sprigs

Melt butter in a saucepan over medium heat. Stir in brown sugar, port, berries, cinnamon, and thyme. The amount of sugar will depend on the sweetness of the berries. Bring to a boil, then reduce the heat to medium and simmer, uncovered, until the liquid is reduced by 1/3 and the berries are tender (about 25 minutes). Remove and discard the cinnamon stick and thyme sprigs.

This is a great topping for
pancakes, waffles, ice cream
and much much more.

Port Caramelized Bacon
Inspired by a friend

Makes 8 Servings
1 pound applewood smoked bacon slices or thick-cut bacon slices
1/2 cup packed brown sugar
1/3 cup of Meyer Family Port
1/2 teaspoon nutmeg
Dash of cream of tartar

Position 1 rack in top third of oven and preheat to 400°F. Line large rimmed baking sheet with foil. Place large rack on lined baking sheet. Arrange bacon slices in single layer on rack.

Add brown sugar, port, nutmeg and cream of tartar to a small saucepan and stir occasionally until mixture has bubbling foam on top and has a brown tone, about 10 minutes. Brush bacon with caramel mixture.

Bake until bacon is crisp and glazed, 15 to 18 minutes. Cool 5 minutes and serve.

Portified Waffles & Pancakes
Inspired by a friend

Makes 4 Servings
4 waffles or 8 pancakes
Port Chantilly
Port Candied Pecans, chopped
Port Berry Compote

Over freshly cooked waffles or pancakes, put desired amount of chopped pecans, port whipped cream and berry compote or syrup.

Desi's Drunken Raspberry Crumb Cake
From the Kitchen of Desiree Gallagher

Makes 12 Servings
Crumbly Sweet Topping
1 cup all-purpose flour
2/3 cup granulated sugar
Grated zest of 1 lemon
1/2 cup unsalted butter, melted

The Cake
3-1/2 cups frouncesen raspberries
250 ml of Meyer Family Port
1-3/4 cup all-purpose flour
1 cup granulated sugar
2 teaspoons baking powder
1/4 teaspoon baking soda
1/4 teaspoon salt
2 large eggs
1 cup sour cream
1 teaspoon vanilla extract
2 tablespoons Confectioner's sugar

Drunken Raspberry

Place frouncesen raspberries in medium bowl, pour the Meyer Family Port over the top. Set aside, soak the raspberries until they are good and drunk , about 20 minutes.

Preheat the oven to 350 F (180 C). Grease and flour an 8x8 pan.

Crumble the Sweet Topping

Stir together the flour, sugar and zest in a small bowl. Add the melted butter and stir with a fork until the mixture is crumbly. Set aside.

The Cake

In a bowl, stir together the flour, sugar, baking powder, baking soda and salt.

In another bowl, whisk together the eggs, sour cream, and vanilla until well blended. Make a well in the center of the dry ingredients and add the sour cream mixture. Beat until smooth and fluffy, about 2 minutes.

Spoon in the batter into the prepared pan and spread evenly. Drain the raspberries and evenly cover the top with raspberries. Sprinkle the crumb topping evenly over the berries.

Bake until the topping is golden brown, 40-45 minutes. Ensure cake is cooked all the way through, by inserting a toothpick in the center of the cake, it should come out clean. Transfer the pan to a wire rack and let cool for 20 minutes.

Dust with confectioners' sugar …..and Enjoy!

Mushroom and Gruyere Bread Pudding

Makes 12 Servings
2 tablespoons olive oil
5 shallots, thinly sliced
1 pound assorted fresh mushrooms,
2 cup of Meyer Family Port
1/2 cup dried porcini mushrooms,
broken into pieces
2 garlic cloves, minced sea salt and
fresh cracked pepper
2 cups whole milk
4 large eggs
1/2 teaspoon salt
1/2 teaspoon ground black pepper
1 loaf of french bread (cubed)
1 cup grated Gruyère cheese
1 cup freshly grated Parmesan cheese

Grease 13x9x2-inch glass baking dish with extra olive oil. Preheat oven to 350°F.

Heat oil in a large nonstick skillet over medium-high heat. Sauté shallots for about 1 minute in skillet. Add thinly sliced assorted mushrooms and sauté for about 3 minutes. Add dried porcini; sauté until mushrooms are brown, about 8 minutes. Add 1 cup of port and garlic and continue to sauté over medium heat until port and mushroom liquor is reduced to about ½ cup. Season with salt and pepper and transfer to medium bowl.

Add 1 cup of port to same skillet; boil until reduced by half, stirring, about 1 minute. Whisk milk and eggs in large bowl to blend. Whisk in port, 1/2 teaspoon salt, and 1/2 teaspoon pepper. Arrange half of the bread cubes over bottom of prepared dish. Top with mushroom mixture, half of Gruyère, and half of Parmesan cheese. Cover with remaining bread cubes. Drizzle egg mixture over; press gently to submerge bread. Sprinkle remaining Gruyère and Parmesan cheese over bread pudding. Bake uncovered until bread pudding puffs and top is golden brown, about 40 minutes.

{IV} Simple Recipes

Port Chantilly

Tipsy Fruit Salad

Raspberries in Port

Sliced Strawberries in Port

Drunken Cantaloupe

Jerry's Figs with Crème Fraiche

Portified Ice Cream

Soaked Pound Cake

 **Port Chantilly**

Makes 2 Cups
2 cups fresh whipping cream
2 tablespoons of Meyer Family Port
1 tablespoon confectioner's sugar

Chill medium mixing bowl in freezer for 10 minutes. Add cream to medium mixing bowl and blend with mixer or whisk until it begins to foam and thicken. Add port and sugar and continue to whisk until soft peaks form. Do not over-whip.

ᵧᵧᵧᵧᵧ Tipsy Fruit Salad

Makes 6 Serving
1 melon, cubed
4 cups assorted berries
2 pears, cored and cubed
1-1/2 cups of Meyer Family Port

Place fruit into medium mixing bowl. Add port and let sit for 10 minutes. Serve and Enjoy.

Raspberries in Port
Inspired by a friend

Makes 1 Cups
3/4 pound raspberries
1 cup of **Meyer Family Port**

Place ripe raspberries in a small mixing bowl. Pour port over berries. Cover and chill for 1 hour, stirring occasionally.

Sliced Strawberries in Port
Inspired by a friend

Makes 3 Cups
3 cups of sliced strawberries
1/4 cup sugar
1 tablespoon of lemon juice
1/2 cup of Meyer Family Port

In mixing bowl, combine sliced strawberries sugar, lemon juice and port and stir.

Chef's Notes
Suggestion: Serve over French
   Toast or Pancakes.
See Strawberry Short Cake

Drunken Cantaloupe

Makes 4 Servings
2 small French cantaloupes
Meyer Family Port

Cut Cantaloupes in half and clean out seeds. Fill core with port and serve.

This recipe is a traditional French Summer Delicacy!

Jerry's Tipsy Figs with Crème Fraiche

From the Kitchen of Jerry Gleeson

Makes 4 Cups
12 fresh figs
Meyer Family Port
6 ounces crème fraiche
1/4 cup brown sugar

Wash figs and cut off stems, keep to expose a whole into the core of the fig big enough to pour in port, but small enough to keep in tact. Place figs base down (cut side up) in 8x8 pan or rimmed dish. Fill fig through cut side with port. Cover and chill for 1 hour. Dip in crème fraiche and then dip in brown sugar and serve.

Portified Ice Cream

Makes 1 Serving
Vanilla Ice Cream
3 tablespoons of Meyer Family Port

Place (2) scoops of vanilla ice cream into bowl. Drizzle port over ice cream and serve.

Soaked Pound Cake
Inspired by a friend

Makes 1 Serving
Pound Cake
Meyer Family Port

Slice pound cake and place on serving dishes. Drizzle port over pound cake and serve.

{V} Sauces

Port Balsamic Vinaigrette

Sweet Port Sauce

Port Barbecue Sauce

Chocolate Barbecue Sauce

Port Balsamic Glaze

Port-Currant Sauce

Cin's Cranberry Sauce with Port & Dried Figs

Port Reduction

Port Tomato Sauce

Port Raspberry Sauce

Port Balsamic Vinaigrette

Makes 1/3 Cup

2 tablespoons of Meyer Family Port
1 tablespoon balsamic vinegar
1 tablespoon extra virgin olive oil
1/2 teaspoon chopped fresh thyme
1-1/2 teaspoons light-colored corn syrup
1/8 teaspoon salt
Dash freshly ground black pepper

Combine all ingredients and stir well before serving or topping on salad.

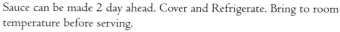 Sweet Port Sauce

Makes 1 Cup
2 cups of Meyer Family Port
1/2 cups sugar
1 tablespoon water
2 teaspoons cornstarch

Stir Port and sugar in heavy small saucepan over low heat until sugar dissolves. Increase heat to medium-high and boil until mixture is reduced to 1 cup, about 13 minutes. Mix water and cornstarch in small bowl. Whisk into Port mixture and boil until slightly thickened, stirring constantly, about 1 minute. Cool.

Chef's Notes
Sauce can be made 2 day ahead. Cover and Refrigerate. Bring to room temperature before serving.

Port Barbecue Sauce

Makes about 1-1/4 cups
1/4 cup of Meyer Family Port
1/4 cup soy sauce
1/4 Dijon mustard
1/4 cup tomato sauce
1/4 cup (packed) brown sugar
3 scallions, finely chopped
1 tablespoon minced fresh rosemary

In a bowl, stir together all ingredients.

Port Chocolate Barbecue Sauce

Makes 1 Cup
2 tablespoons of vegetable oil
4 shallots, chopped
1 cup of Meyer Family Port
3 tablespoons butter
2 tablespoons (packed) light brown sugar
2 tablespoons balsamic vinegar
2 tablespoons minced fresh Rosemary
1 cup finely chopped/grated dark chocolate

Heat saucepan on high heat. Sauté shallots in vegetable oil until tender. Add 1 cup Port, butter, sugar, vinegar and rosemary. Cover and bring to boil. Reduce heat to medium and cook, covered, for 15 minutes. Add chocolate and stir until melted.

Remove from heat. Season to taste with salt and pepper. Serve warm.

Chef's Notes
Sauce can be made 1 day ahead. Cover and Refrigerate
When reheating, add more port by tablespoonfuls if the mixture is dry.

Port Balsamic Glaze

Makes 1 Cup
2 tablespoons of vegetable oil
4 shallots, chopped
1 cup of Meyer Family Port
3 tablespoons butter
2 tablespoons (packed) light
brown sugar
2 tablespoons balsamic vinegar
3 teaspoons minced fresh thyme

Heat saucepan on high heat. Sauté shallots in vegetable oil until tender. Add I cup Port, butter, sugar, vinegar and thyme. Cover and bring to boil. Reduce heat to medium and cook, covered, 15 minutes.

Remove from heat. Season to taste with salt and pepper. Serve warm.

Chef's Notes
Sauce can be made 1 day ahead. Cover and Refrigerate.
When reheating, add more port by tablespoonfuls if the mixture is dry.

Port-Currant Sauce

Makes about 3/4 cup
2 tablespoons vegetable oil
3 shallots, chopped
1 medium Granny Smith apple,
unpeeled, cored, chopped
2 garlic cloves, chopped
750-ml (1-1/2 bottles) of Meyer
Family Port
1 cup chicken stock or canned low-
salt chicken broth
1/3 cup dried currants

Heat oil in heavy medium saucepan over medium-high heat. Add onion, apple and garlic; sauté until onion is tender and golden, about 12 minutes. Add Port; reduce heat to medium. Simmer until mixture is reduced to 2 cups, about 30 minutes. Strain mixture; return liquid to saucepan. Discard solids in strainer. Add stock to saucepan; simmer until liquid is reduced to 3/4 cup, about 15 minutes. Stir in currants. Season sauce to taste with salt and pepper.

Chef's Notes
Can be made 1 day ahead. Cover and chill. Rewarm over low heat.

Cin's Cranberry Sauce with Port & Dried Fruit

From the Kitchen of Cindy Moon

Makes about 3 cups
1 - 2/3 cup Meyer Family Port
1/4 cup balsamic vinegar
1/4 cup packed brown sugar
8 dried black Mission figs, stemmed and chopped
1 (6 inch long) sprig of fresh rosemary
1/4 teaspoon fresh ground black pepper
1 (12 ounces) bag of fresh cranberries
3/4 cup sugar

Combine the first 6 ingredients in a medium saucepan Bring to a boil, stirring until sugar dissolves. Reduce heat to low and simmer for 10 minutes. Discard rosemary. Mix in cranberries and sugar. Cook over medium heat until liquid is slightly reduced and berries burst, about 6 minutes. Chill.

Port Reduction

Makes about 1/2 cup
500 ml (1 bottle) of Meyer Family Port
1/2 cup superfine granulated sugar
1-1/2 teaspoons whole black peppercorns
2 fresh mint leaves, torn into bits

Bring Port, superfine sugar, peppercorns, and mint to a simmer in a medium saucepan over low heat, stirring until sugar is dissolved. Remove from heat, then carefully ignite Port with a kitchen match, letting flames die down (this will take a few minutes). Simmer over low heat until sauce is thickened and reduced to about 1/2 cup, about 15 minutes. Transfer to a medium bowl.

Port Tomato Sauce
Inspired by a friend

Makes 1 Cup
1 tablespoon of olive oil
1 cup chopped white onion
2 cloves minced garlic
2 tablespoons chopped oregano
5 roma tomatoes, diced
1 tablespoon tomato paste
1/2 cup of Meyer Family Port
salt and pepper to taste

Heat olive oil in saucepan on medium heat. Add onions and cook until tender. Add garlic and oregano and stir and add diced tomatoes and tomato paste and port. Add salt and pepper to taste. Turn down heat to simmer for 30 minutes to blend.

Port Raspberry Sauce

Makes about 1-1/4 cups
1/4 cup of Meyer Family Port
1 cup fresh raspberry puree
sugar to taste

Blend all ingredients in a blender. Add sugar to taste.

{VI} Appetizers

Baked Figs
Fig and Goat Cheese Crostini
Roasted Portobello Crostini
Lala's Meatball Appetizer
Jerry's Cocktail Sausages
Kels' Tomato and Goat Cheese Flatbread
Baked Oysters

Baked Figs

Makes 10 Servings
10 fresh Figs, halved
10 ounces Goat Cheese
6 ounces Prosciutto
1/2 cup Balsamic Glaze

Preheat the oven to 400°F. Halve each fig lengthways through the stalk. Place the figs in a baking sheet or in a baking dish. Place a small spoon full of goat cheese on each half, and wrap fig in half of a slice of prosciutto. Bake for 15-20 minutes, or until prosciutto is crisp. Top with Balsamic Glaze and serve warm.

Fig and Goat Cheese Crostini
Inspired by a friend

Makes 24 Hors d'Oeuvres
3 tablespoons minced shallot
2 (3-inch) fresh thyme sprigs plus
1/2 teaspoon minced fresh thyme
1/2 bay leaf
1-1/2 tablespoons unsalted butter
3/4 cup dried Black Mission figs,
finely chopped
3/4 cup of Meyer Family Port
1/4 teaspoon salt
1/8 teaspoon black pepper
12 (1/2-inch thick) diagonally cut
baguette slices
1 tablespoon olive oil
6 ounces soft mild goat cheese

Garnish: fresh thyme leaves
2 Fresh Figs

Cook shallot, thyme sprigs, and bay leaf in butter in a heavy small saucepan over medium heat, stirring, until shallot is softened, about 2 minutes. Add dried figs, Port, salt, and pepper and bring to a boil. Cover and simmer until figs are soft, about 10 minutes. If there is still liquid in saucepan, remove lid and simmer, stirring, until most of liquid is evaporated, 3 to 4 minutes more. Discard bay leaf and thyme sprigs and transfer jam to a bowl. Cool, then stir in minced thyme and salt and pepper to taste.

Make toasts while jam cools. Preheat to 350°F. Slice baguette diagonally. Place on a baking sheet and brush tops lightly with oil. Bake until lightly toasted, about 7 minutes. Cool on baking sheet on a rack.

Spread each toast with 1-1/2 teaspoons goat cheese and top with 1 teaspoon fig jam. Garnish with thyme leaves and slice of fresh fig.

Roasted Portobello Crostini
Inspired by a friend

Makes 20 Servings
3 large portobello mushrooms caps
3/4 cup port balsamic vinaigrette,
plus 2 tablespoons divided
2 tablespoons olive oil
1 cup herb goat cheese
1 Rustic Tuscan Loaf
1/2 cup roasted red bell pepper, cut
into 1/2-inch wide strips
Fresh oregano leaves,
Salt and freshly ground black pepper

Preheat oven to 400°F. Cut Tuscan loaf into thin slices, place on cookie sheet and bake in oven for 10 minutes or until toasted/golden brown. Put crostini aside for later.

Clean portobello mushroom caps. Cut into 1/2-inch slices, place in a large zip-top bag and add 3/4 cup of port balsamic vinaigrette. Squeeze air from bag and seal. Lightly massage the mushrooms to ensure they are all evenly coated. Marinate in refrigerator for 1 hour.

Heat olive oil in a large saute pan over medium/high heat. Add the marinated mushrooms and saute for about 6 to 8 minutes until tender.

Spread crostini with the goat cheese mixture. Top each crostini with a portobello slice and cross with a red pepper strip. Garnish with oregano leaf and salt and pepper.

Lala's Meatball Appetizer
From the Kitchen of Sheila McNamara

Makes 12 Servings
Meatballs
1 pound. ground beef
1/2 pound. pork sausage
1 egg
2 tablespoons Meyer Family Port
2 tablespoons of olive oil

Sauce
2 shallots, chopped
2-1/2 cup tawny port
1-1/2 cup water
2 tablespoons balsamic vinegar
fresh rosemary
fresh thyme
salt and pepper

Mix all meatball ingredients together well. Shape into 3/4 inch meatballs. Brown well in olive oil and set aside.

Saute shallots in drippings from meatball browning, until lightly browned. Add port, water, and balsamic vinegar. Simmer for about 1/2 hour. Add herbs, salt, and pepper to taste.

Add meatballs and simmer over low heat covered for 1/2 hour. Remove cover, and continue to simmer until liquid has thickened and coated meatballs well, about 1/2 hour more.

Portobello Tomato Bruschetta

Makes 4 Servings
3 large portobello mushrooms caps
3/4 cup port balsamic vinaigrette
1 Rustic Tuscan Loaf
2 tablespoons finely minced garlic
extra-virgin olive oil
4 ripe roma tomatoes, diced
3/4 cup coarsely chopped fresh basil
salt and pepper to taste

Clean portobello mushroom caps. Place in a large zip-top bag and add 3/4 cup of port balsamic vinaigrette. Squeeze air from bag and seal. Lightly massage the mushrooms to ensure they are all evenly coated. Marinate in refrigerator for 1 hour.

Preheat oven to 400°F. Cut Tuscan loaf into thick slices, place on cookie sheet. Drizzle olive oil on each slice and spread a 1/4-1/2 of a clove of minced garlic on each slice and bake in oven for 10 minutes or until toasted/golden brown. Put crostini aside for later.

In a bowl, mix tomatoes and basil. Add salt and pepper to taste.

Heat grill pan over medium heat. Reserving vinaigrette. Place mushrooms on grill pan and cook until desired doneness. Place mushrooms on top of the garlic crostini and top with tomato mixture and add tablespoon of vinaigrette to each.

Kels' Tomato and Goat Cheese Flatbread
From the Kitchen of Kelsey Gallagher

Makes 3 (7-inch)
Diameter Pies
Pizza dough
1 cup warm water (85-110°F)
1 tablespoons active dry yeast
(from 1 envelope)
1 tablespoon salt
4 cups all purpose flour (plus 1
cup for rolling out dough)
2 tablespoons olive oil

Flatbread topping
1 cup of port tomato sauce,
divided
8 ounces goat cheese
1/4 cup fresh oregano

Pizza dough
Pour warm water into small bowl; sprinkle yeast over. Let stand until yeast dissolves, about 20 minutes. Put flour and salt in large bowl and add yeast. Stir until dough forms. Knead dough until smooth, adding more flour if very sticky, about 6 minutes. Coat large bowl with olive oil; add dough to the center of the bowl. Cover bowl with damp kitchen towel. Let dough rise in warm draft-free area until doubled, about 1 hour.

Divide dough into 2 equal portions. Transfer to floured surface and roll out each to 9-inch round. Transfer to prepared baking sheets. Let stand while preparing topping. Preheat oven to 450°F.

Flatbread topping
Distribute port tomato sauce amongst flatbread. Evenly distribute crumbled goat cheese and fresh oregano leaves. Bake until golden and beginning to crisp, about 17 minutes.

Baked Oysters

Makes 4-6 Servings

2 dozen oysters, shucked and drained

1-1/2 to 2 cups port tomato sauce

1 cup Parmesan cheese, grated

Preheat the oven to 425°F. Shuck and drain the oysters. Layout in one layer on a cookie sheet. Add a tablespoon of port tomato sauce to each oyster and a large pinch of Parmesan cheese on top of the tomato sauce. Place oysters in the oven for 10-12 minutes.

{VII} Sides

Mama Meyer's Mushrooms
Grilled Asparagus
Asparagus & Prosciutto
Grilled Pears with Blackberry Port Sauce
Grilled Peaches with Sweet Port Sauce
Lala's Grilled Tomatoes
Onions with Currant, Port and Balsamic Glaze
Pear & Pecan Salad with Port Vinaigrette
Pat's Pumpkin Marble Soup

Mama Meyer's Mushrooms
From the Kitchen of Bonny Meyer

Makes 10 Servings
2 to 3 tablespoons Olive Oil
5 shallots, thinly sliced
3 large portobello mushrooms, sliced
1 clove garlic, minced
1 cup of Meyer Family Port
sea salt and fresh cracked pepper

Sauté shallots in olive oil on high heat in a large skillet, about one minute. Add mushrooms and brown, about (1) 2 minutes. Add garlic and port and continue to sauté over medium heat until port and mushroom liquor is reduced to about ½ cup. Season the mushrooms with salt and pepper, to taste.

Chef's Notes
*Suggestion – Serve with Tenderloin Steak with Port Sauce.

Grilled Asparagus

Makes 6 to 8 Servings
2 bunches Asparagus
Olive Oil
Fresh ground salt and pepper
Port Balsamic Glaze

Heat up grill to medium heat. Clean asparagus and snap off bottoms. Drizzle olive oil over asparagus and generously grind black pepper and salt. Mix so that asparagus is evenly coated with olive oil and seasoning. Place on grill and cook until desired doneness.

Serve and drizzle with Port Balsamic Glaze.

Asparagus & Prosciutto

Makes 6 to 8 Servings
2 bunches Asparagus
10 ounces Goat Cheese
Port Balsamic Glaze
6 ounces Prosciutto

Preheat the oven to 400°F. Clean asparagus and snap off bottoms. Add a quarter sized chunk of goat cheese to three spears of asparagus and add a splash of port balsamic glaze to the goat cheese. Adhere goat cheese to asparagus by wrapping goat cheese against spear with prosciutto, so that top and goat cheese is not visible. Place asparagus on cookie sheet and place in oven for 15-20 minutes, or until prosciutto is crisp.

Optional: Drizzle with Port Balsamic Glaze.

Grilled Pears with Blackberry Port Sauce
Inspired by winemaker brother, Matt Meyer

Makes 8 Servings
1 cup blackberries
1 cup of Meyer Family Port
3 tablespoons sugar
1 (3-inch) cinnamon stick
2 fresh thyme springs
1/4 teaspoon red pepper flakes

4 large pears, peeled, cored, and halved

In a small saucepan over medium heat, combine the blackberries, port, sugar, cinnamon, thyme, and red pepper flakes. The amount of sugar will depend on the sweetness of the berries. Bring to a boil, then reduce the heat to medium and simmer, uncovered, until the liquid is reduced by 1/3 and the berries are tender, about 25 minutes. Remove and discard the cinnamon stick and thyme sprigs. Transfer the contents of the pan to a blender and puree until smooth. Strain through a fine-mesh sieve into a bowl and set aside.

In a medium bowl, toss the pears with the olive oil. Place on the hottest part of the grill rack, turning until there are light grill marks on each of the pear wedges, about 3 minutes. Remove. Cover pears with sauce and serve.

*"This is a summer family favorite of ours.
Toss them in olive oil, place them on the
grill, and fill them with port. Done."*

- Matt Meyer

Grilled Peaches with Sweet Port Sauce
Inspired by winemaker brother, Matt Meyer

Makes 8 Servings
1 cup of **Meyer Family Port**
1/4 cup sugar
3 teaspoons water
1 teaspoon cornstarch
4 ripe peaches, halved and pitted
Olive oil

Stir Port and sugar in heavy small saucepan over low heat until sugar dissolves. Increase heat to medium-high and boil until mixture is reduced to 1/2 cup, about 13 minutes. Mix water and cornstarch in small bowl. Whisk into Port mixture and boil until slightly thickened, stirring constantly, about 1 minute. Cool. (Can be made 2 days ahead. Cover and chill. Bring to room temperature before serving.)

Heat up grill. Cut peaches in half and take out the pit. Rub peaches in olive oil and place on grill for 3-4 minutes each side (or until there are grill marks on the peaches). Take peaches off the grill and drizzle port sauce over the top.

Lala's Grilled Tomatoes
From the Kitchen of Sheila McNamara

Makes 4 Servings
4 hot house tomatoes
500 ml (1 bottle) of Meyer
Family Port
4 ounces gorgonzola cheese
Salt and pepper

Wash tomatoes and thinly slice off stem end. Fill tomatoes will port and place in refrigerator to marinade for (1) 2 hours. Heat up grill to medium heat. Drain port and set aside. Place tomatoes open side down on grill, cook for 5 minutes. Flip tomatoes, fill with port, top with gorgonzola, salt and pepper. Close lid and cook until cheese is melted.

Onions with Currant Port Balsamic Glaze
Inspired by a friend

Makes 6 to 8 Servings
2 pounds small boiling onions
(about 3/4 to 1 inch in diameter)
1 cup Meyer Family Port
2/3 cup dried currants
3 tablespoons butter
2 tablespoons (packed) light
brown sugar
2 tablespoons balsamic vinegar
3 teaspoons minced fresh thyme

Cook onions in large pot of boiling salted water 2 minutes to loosen skins. Drain and cool slightly. Cut root ends from onions. Peel onions. (Can be prepared 1 day ahead. Cover and refrigerate.)

Combine onions, 1 cup Port, currants, butter, sugar, 1 tablespoon vinegar and 2 teaspoons thyme in heavy large skillet. Cover and bring to boil. Reduce heat to medium and cook, covered, 15 minutes. Uncover and cook until onions are almost tender and coated with glaze, stirring frequently, about 10 minutes. Remove from heat. Mix in remaining 1 tablespoon vinegar. Season to taste with salt and pepper. Sprinkle with remaining 1 teaspoon thyme and serve.

Pear & Pecan Salad with Goat Cheese and Port Vinaigrette

Makes 4 Servings
Port Vinaigrette
1 (5-1/2 ounce) bag mixed salad greens
2 port poached pears, sliced
5 ounces fresh goat cheese, crumbled
1/2 cup dried cranberries
1 cup port candied pecans

In salad bowl, combine salad greens, prosciutto, pear slices, goat cheese, dried cranberries and walnuts. Add fresh cracked salt and pepper to taste. Add port vinaigrette and toss together.

"This is a great fall soup, especially if you have a vegetable garden. A harvest feast! It's possible to substitute or even add more circles, if you think of more colorful soups or add a drop of cream in the middle."

- Pat Gentenaar

Pat's Pumpkin Marble Soup
From the Kitchen of Pat Gentenaar

Makes 10 Servings

5 garlic cloves, crushed, divided into 2 piles
4 tablespoon olive oil
2 onions, peeled and chopped
4-1/2 pound pumpkin, peeled, seeded and cut into 1 inch dice
1 tablespoon mild curry powder
2 teaspoon salt
1/2 cup sugared ginger
2 cup vegetable stock, split
1/2 cup of cream
2-1/2 pound diced potatoes
2 pound leeks, sliced in 1 inch pieces
1 pound broccoli florets
2 tablespoon flat-leaf parsley
2 tablespoon flat-leaf celery
1 teaspoon salt
1 teaspoon freshly ground black pepper
1/2 cup of cream
1 pound goat cream cheese
20 Medjoul dates, pitted
3/4 cup roasted pine nuts
1 young beet
1-1/2 cups Meyer Family Port

Also good without the cream
Optional: Add thin bacon

First Circle
In a large cast iron pan, fry the peeled and chopped onions. When they start to brown, add the diced pumpkin, curry powder, salt and stock. Cover and slowly cook the pumpkin, stirring regularly. When it's almost soft, add half of the garlic and the ginger. Cook 5 more minutes and blend the soup with a staff mixer while adding the cream.

Second Circle Can be made a day in advance.
While the pumpkin is cooking, put the potatoes in a large soup pan first with the bouillon and then add water until the potatoes are submerged. As they are coming up to a boil and add the leeks, broccoli florets, flat-leaf parsley, flat-leaf celery, salt and pepper. When the potatoes are almost soft, add the second half of the garlic. Cook 5 more minutes. Do not drain. Blend the soup with a staff mixer while adding the cream.

Third Circle
Roast the pine nuts. Cook the beet: either boil it or put it in the microwave for 3 minutes, possibly 2 times. Check with a fork to make sure it is cooked through. Cut it into half inch dice. Cut the dates into fours. Put the goat cream cheese, pine nuts, beet and dates in a blender or food processor and blend, slowly adding the Port. Optional / additional: make in advance and pass around with the soup for an optional garnish. Render* the fat out of the thin sliced bacon, drain and crumble it. *Put a few drops of olive oil in a frying pan. Take the bacon and slice it the other direction too, so that you can drop small pieces into the pan. Cook it slowly, stirring regularly until the fat is transparent and the meat has become crispy.

This works best in a wide soup bowl. Pour the pumpkin soup in first, leaving space for the next two circles. Then pour the second circle gently in the middle. The Port circle then goes carefully in the middle. When you mix it with your spoon you can make wonderful marble patterns!

{VIII} Main Dishes

Gruyère, Prosciutto and Pear Pizza with Spring Greens
Roast Beef Tenderlion with Port Sauce
Rosemary Burgers with Port Balsamic Glaze
Braised Short Ribs
Captain Fantastic's Swedish Meatballs
Seared Duck Breast
Celia's Receta de Mole
Norma's Beet, Cherry and Port Risotto
Menashe's Drunken Noodles

Gruyère, Prosciutto and Pear Pizza with Spring Greens

Makes (3) 7" Diameter Pies
Pizza dough
1-1/3 cups warm water (85-110°F)
1 tablespoons active dry yeast
(from 1 envelope)
1 teaspoon sugar
1 tablespoon salt
4 cups all purpose flour (plus 1
cup for rolling out dough)
2 tablespoons olive oil

Pizza topping
6 tablespoons olive oil, divided
3 cups thinly sliced Port Poached
Pears
6 ounces sliced prosciutto, torn
into strips
3 cups (packed) grated Gruyère
cheese
2 cups Spring Greens

Pizza dough
Pour warm water into small bowl; sprinkle yeast over and sugar. Let stand until yeast dissolves, about 20 minutes. Put flour and salt in large bowl and add yeast. Stir until dough forms. Knead dough until smooth, adding more flour if very sticky, about 6 minutes.

Coat large bowl with olive oil; add dough to the center of the bowl. Cover bowl with damp kitchen towel. Let dough rise in warm draft-free area until doubled, about 1 hour.

Divide dough into 3 equal portions. Transfer to floured surface and roll out each to 7-inch round. Transfer to prepared baking sheets. Brush dough with olive oil. Let stand while preparing topping. Preheat oven to 450°F.

Pizza topping
Divide sliced poached pears, prosciutto, and Gruyère among pizza crusts. Bake until golden and beginning to crisp, about 17 minutes. Divide Spring Greens among pizzas.

The crust is a Justin Meyer original. The toppings are a nice combination of salty and sweet.

Roast Beef Tenderlion with Port Sauce
Inspired by a friend

Makes 10 servings
Beef
1 (4 to 5 pound) trimmed whole
beef tenderloin, tied every 3 inches
2 teaspoons coarse kosher salt

Sauce
4 tablespoons (1/2 stick) chilled
unsalted butter, divided
1/4 cup finely chopped shallots
3 tablespoons brandy
1 fresh rosemary sprig
1 teaspoon black pepper
1 cup of Meyer Family Port
3 cups of Beef Stock

Sprinkle beef tenderloin with coarse sea salt. Place beef on rack set over large rimmed baking sheet. Refrigerate uncovered at least 24 hours.

Melt 2 tablespoons butter in large saucepan over medium-low heat. Add shallots; sauté until soft, 3 minutes. Add brandy, rosemary, and 1 teaspoon cracked pepper and cook until liquid evaporates, 1 minute. Add Port; bring to simmer. Add all of beef stock. Boil until reduced to 1-1/2 cups, about 20 minutes. Strain into medium saucepan, pressing on solids to extract as much liquid as possible. Discard solids in strainer.

Let beef stand at room temperature 1 hour before roasting. Position rack in center of oven and preheat to 425°F. Rub beef all over with oil; sprinkle with 2 tablespoons cracked peppercorns, pressing to adhere. Return beef to rack on baking sheet and roast until meat is 125°F for medium-rare, about 30 minutes. Remove roast from oven and let rest 15 minutes.

Bring sauce to boil; whisk in remaining 2 tablespoons butter. Season sauce to taste with salt and pepper.

Cut off string from roast. Cut roast crosswise into 1/2-inch-thick slices and serve with sauce.

Rosemary Burgers with Port Balsamic Glaze
Inspired by a friend

Makes 4 Servings
Hamburger Patties
1 pound ground beef
1/2 teaspoon crushed dried
rosemary
1 pinch salt
1 pinch pepper
1/4 teaspoon garlic powder
2 tablespoons of Port
Balsamic Glaze
2 tablespoons butter

Hamburger Fixings
Port Balsamic Glaze
4 ciabatta sandwich rolls (cut in
half – toasted if desired)
1-1/2 cups of crumbled gorgonzola
cheese
2 cups spring greens

Preheat a grill for high heat.

In a medium bowl, mix together the ground beef, rosemary, salt, pepper and garlic powder. Divide the mixture into four parts and form into balls. Make an indention in the center of each one, and place a tablespoon of butter in the hole. Mold the meat around the butter, and flatten into a patty.

Lightly oil the grilling surface, and place burgers on the preheated grill. Cook for 5 to 10 minutes on each side, until well done. Melt gorgonzola over first finished side and cook while other side is cooking.

Lightly dip cut ciabatta bread (toast if desired) into Port Balsamic Glaze. Fix hamburgers with spring greens; and excess port balsamic glaze, if desired.

Braised Short Ribs

Makes 6 Servings
3 slices applewood bacon, chopped
6 pounds bone-in short ribs
1/2 cup white onion, finely chopped
5 large shallots, finely chopped
1/4 cup celery, finely chopped
1/4 cup carrots, peeled and finely chopped
3 minced garlic cloves
2-1/2 cups of Meyer Family Port
3 cups chicken broth
2 cups drained canned diced tomatoes
2 large fresh thyme sprig
1 bay leaf

5 tablespoons finely chopped dark chocolate
1 teaspoon finely chopped fresh rosemary

Heat heavy large pot over medium heat. Add bacon and sauté until crisp. Using slotted spoon, transfer bacon to paper towels to drain. Sprinkle ribs with salt and pepper. Working in batches, brown ribs in drippings in pot over medium-high heat until brown on all sides, about 8 minutes per batch. Transfer to plate.

Add onions and next 4 ingredients to pot. Cover, reduce heat to medium, and cook until vegetables are soft, stirring occasionally, about 10 minutes. Add port. Boil uncovered until liquid is reduced by half, scraping up browned bits, about 5 minutes. Add broth, tomatoes, thyme, bay leaf, and bacon. Return ribs to pot, cover partially, and simmer 1-1/2 hours. Uncover and simmer until rib meat is tender, stirring occasionally, about 1-1/2 hours longer.

Transfer ribs to plate and cover. Discard the bay leaf, spoon fat from surface of sauce, and boil sauce until beginning to thicken, about 8 minutes. Reduce heat to medium. Add chocolate and rosemary; stir until chocolate melts. Season to taste with salt and pepper. Return the ribs to the pot and simmer to rewarm, about 5 minutes.

Ruggero's *Filetto con Fichi* (Filet with Fig Sauce)
From the Kitchen of Chef Ruggero Gigli

Makes 8 Servings
8 fresh black figs, or 12 dried black figs, chopped finely
1/2 cup pine nuts, chopped finely
4 garlic cloves, chopped finely
1/2 pound unsalted butter
1 cup of Meyer Family Port
8 steak filets, all fat trimmed off

For *Salsa al Fico* (Fig Sauce), stir ingredients together in the top of a bagnomaria - double boiler - and simmer over hot water for 30 minutes.

Grill steaks over very hot heat for three minutes each side for medium-rare. Place each filet on a warmed plate and pout hot *Salsa al Fico* over.

"This sauce came about when Gina and I lived in Napa Valley, and some good friends who had a beautiful fig tree on their property gave us a bucket of ripe black figs. I figured I had to do something with all of those figs. The two of us certainly couldn't eat them all. I had been asked by Sterling Vineyards to cater a lunch for 60 people in the vineyards, so I created a larger version of this sauce and poured it over 60 steaks. Filetto con Fichi has since become the favorite speciale on our Villa Gigli menu."

- Ruggero Gigli

"Meatballs are a classic family dinner dish that can be found in various forms from cultures throughout Europe. The type of meat is not of prime concern and although this recipe calls for beef and lamb in equal proportions, this can be changed to suit your needs, desires and taste buds.

What is important, is the method of serving. No matter whether you, the host, are dishing up, or the meal is served family style. It is very important to the spirit of the dish that each member should; on their own plate, mash the boiled potatoes with a fork and apply a desired amount of butter. (This, coincidentally, separates the men from the boys, where the men mash their own potatoes, but the boys, and other children, have an adult assist them). Last to the plate are the meatballs and sauce.

The placement of meatballs in relation to the potatoes already on the plate are a matter of greatly differing individual preference and of huge importance. Some prefer all meatballs and sauce completely contained on, and in, the mashed potatoes; while others would rather they not touch at all. I myself prefer placing the meatballs to the right of the potatoes, with sauce covering the meatballs completely as well as the nearest 15-20% of the potatoes. This preference should not be taken lightly, for myself or others. Enjoy!"

- Conrad James McGreal

Captain Fantastic's Swedish Meatballs
From the Kitchen of Conrad James McGreal

Makes 4 Servings
3 tablespoons of fresh thyme
1 medium white onion
1/2 pound ground lamb
1/2 pound ground beef
1 egg
1/8 cup of flour
fresh ground sea salt
fresh ground pepper
1 tablespoon of butter
1 cup of Meyer Family Port
1 pint of cream
1 packet of McCormick
Peppercorn Gravy
10 ounces of baby carrots

8-10 small red potatoes
Butter

In a food processor, finely mince onion and thyme together. In a large bowl, combine together by hand the onion, thyme, ground lamb, ground beef, egg, flour, and salt and pepper to taste. Cover meatball mixture with plastic wrap and refrigerate for a minimum of 15 minutes.

In a large saucepan, boil the potatoes for 20-25 minutes. In the meanwhile, roll meat into golf ball sized balls and set aside. Place butter in a non-stick skillet and set to medium heat. Add meatballs to skillet and cook for 5-7 minutes. Add Port and simmer for a minute. Add McCormick Cracked Peppercorn Gravy Mix and cream into the skillet and cook for 5 minutes. Add baby carrots and cook to taste.

Serve meatballs and sauce with lightly buttered boiled potatoes.

Seared Duck Breast with Port Raspberry Sauce
Inspired by a friend

Makes 4 Servings
4 (6 ounce) duck breast halves or
2 (12 ounce) duck breast
4 tablespoons butter
4-5 medium shallots, finely chopped
1 cup chicken broth
20 fresh raspberries
1/3 cup of Meyer Family Port
2 tablespoons of orange blossom honey

Place duck breast halves between 2 sheets of plastic wrap. Pound lightly to even thickness (about 1/2 to 3/4 inch). Discard plastic wrap. Using sharp knife, score skin in 3/4-inch diamond pattern (do not cut into flesh). Can be made 8 hours ahead. Cover and chill.

Melt 1 tablespoon butter in heavy large skillet over medium-high heat. Sprinkle duck with salt and pepper. Add duck, skin side down, to skillet and cook until skin is browned and crisp, about 5 minutes. Turn duck breasts over, reduce heat to medium, and cook until browned and cooked to desired doneness, about 4 minutes longer for small breasts and 8 minutes longer for large breast for medium-rare. Transfer to work surface, tent with foil to keep warm, and let rest 10 minutes.

Meanwhile, pour off all but 2 tablespoons drippings from skillet. Add shallot to skillet and stir over medium heat 30 seconds. Add broth, raspberries, Port, and honey. Increase heat to high and boil until sauce is reduced to glaze, stirring often, about 3 minutes. Whisk in 1 tablespoon butter. Season sauce to taste with salt and pepper.

Thinly slice duck and spoon sauce over and serve.

Celia's Receta de Mole
From the Kitchen of Celia Rios

Makes 4 Servings
3 ounces dry chile pasilla
3 ounces dry chile negro
1/3 cup canola oil, plus 3 tablespoon
1 corn tortilla
5 saltine crackers
3 small French baguette slices
1 medium tomato
1 ripe banana
1 medium white onion
2 medium tomatillos
2 garlic cloves
2 tablespoon pumpkin seeds
2 tablespoon peanuts
2 tablespoon sesame seeds
1 tablespoon chili seeds
Pinch of ground cinnamon
4 whole cloves
1/4 teaspoon dry oregano
1/4 teaspoon cumin
1 bay leaf
1 teaspoon of salt
4 whole allspice
1 ounces Mexican chocolate
Meyer Family Port
1 whole roasted chicken

Split all the chile pods lengthwise and reserve 1 tablespoon of seeds.

Warm the canola oil at medium temperature in medium saucepan. Putting ingredients in one at a time (except for Chocolate and Port) into oil, lightly brown. Make sure you are not burning the chiles while you cook. When all ingredients are cooked, blend in small batches in the blender, use water to help blend. Put the result paste into a strainer.

Clean and dry pot pour and pour the remaining 3 tablespoons of canola oil and put over high temperature. Pour the paste and add the chocolate stir until the chocolate melts. Add salt and port to taste.

Put over roasted chicken.

Menashe's Drunken Noodles
From the Kitchen of Shawn Menashe

Makes 4 Servings
1-1/2 pounds of spaghetti
1 shallot
2 clove garlic
fresh ground sea salt
fresh ground pepper
750 ml (1 bottle) Meyer Family
Cellars Syrah
500 ml (1 bottle) Meyer Family Port
1 bunch broccoli rabe
4 Italian sausages (hot, mild, or
sweet or combo)
Extra virgin olive oil
1 lemon
1 sprig of fresh Rosemary
Parmesan reggiano cheese

In a large pan add tablespoon of extra virgin olive oil and set at medium heat. Add inch segments of sausage and cook until browned. Add sliced garlic and shallots sauté for 2-3 minutes. Then add bite size pieces of broccoli, 1 lemon worth of zest and finely minced Rosemary. Add salt an pepper to taste. Sauté for another 3 minutes and take off heat.

In a large pot boil salted water and once at a rolling boil add pasta. At same time add wine to a deep sauce pan and bring to a rolling boil. After 4 minutes in salted water, strain pasta and add to boiling wine. Stir occasionally until all wine is absorbed and evaporated.

Add sausage mixture into noodles and combine. Add juice from half lemon and drizzle of extra virgin olive oil over to finish. Add more salt and pepper to taste.

Finish with cheese if desired.

Norma's Beet, Cherry and Port Risotto
From the Kitchen of Norma Alcantara

Makes 6 Servings
12 ounces Arborio rice
6 ounces dried sour cherries
1 cup Meyer Family Port
3 tablespoons olive oil
1 large onion, finely chopped
2 celery stalks, finely chopped
1/2 teaspoon dried thyme
1 garlic clove
5 cups chicken
4 cooked beet, diced
2 tablespoons chopped fresh dill
2 tablespoons fresh chives
salt and pepper
1/2 cup grated Parmesan cheese

Place the sour cherries in a pan with port and bring to a boil, reduce the heat and let simmer for 2 minutes until reduced, remove from heat and set aside.

Heat the olive oil in a large, heavy pan over medium heat; add the onion, celery and thyme, stirring until just starting to soften. Add the garlic and cook for 30 seconds. Reduce the heat, add the rice and mix to coat with oil stirring until grains are translucent. Gradually add the stock, stir constantly, add more stock as rice absorbs it. Increase the heat to medium, cook for about 20 minutes until rice is creamy. Halfway through the risotto cooking time, remove the cherries from the port and add to the risotto with the beet and half the port. Continue adding the stock and the wine.

Stir in the dill and chives and season, serve with a garnish of Parmesan.

{IX} Desserts

Candied Pecans
Spiced Port Cookies
Port Ice Cream with Chocolate Chunks
Aunt Evelyn's Cantaloupe Sorbet
Poached Pears
Stuffed Baked Apples
Plum Tart
Apple Raisin Bread Pudding
Strawberry Shortcake
Rhubarb Port Crisp
Candi's Raspberry Crème Brûlée

Candied Pecans

Makes 2 cups
1/2 cup packed brown sugar
1/3 cup of Meyer Family Port
1 teaspoon nutmeg
1 teaspoon cinnamon
dash of cream of tartar
2 cups pecan halves (8 to 9 ounces)

Preheat oven to 300°F. Cover large rimmed baking sheet with foil and brush with butter.

Put pecans in mixing bowl and set aside. Add first 5 ingredients to a small saucepan and stir occasionally until mixture has bubbling foam on top and has a brown tone, about 10 minutes. Pour hot mixture over pecans and stir until pecans are evenly coated. Transfer nuts with a slotted spoon to baking pan (discarding extra syrup).

Bake until golden brown, about 35 minutes. Cool completely on sheet. Transfer to container, cover and store at room temperature.

Chef's Notes
Can be made 4 days ahead.

Tatu's Spiced Port Cookies
From the Kitchen of Victor Woolworth

Makes about 24 cookies
2 cups all purpose flour
1/2 teaspoon baking soda
1/2 teaspoon cream of tartar
1 teaspoon ground cinnamon
1/2 teaspoon ground ginger
1/4 teaspoon ground cloves
1 cup brown sugar
4 ounces chopped almonds
2 eggs (lightly beaten)
1/2 cup of Meyer Family Port
1/2 cup of chilled butter, cut into small slices
1 egg white (beaten)

Preheat oven to 350°F. Lightly grease baking sheet.

Mix together flour, baking soda, cream of tartar, cinnamon, ginger, nutmeg, cloves, brown sugar and almonds in large mixing bowl. Add butter and cut it into the flour mixture. Add the beaten eggs and port and mix the dough together until it can be formed into a ball. Roll dough into 1" balls and place on cookie sheet about 1" apart. Brush each cookie gently with egg white.

Bake for 12-15 minutes, until golden brown. Remove and cool.

Port Ice Cream with Chocolate Chunks

Makes 10 Servings
6 large egg yolks
3/4 cup sugar
2-1/4 cups milk (do not use low-fat or nonfat)
1-1/8 cups whipping cream
1/4 cup Meyer Family Port
2 tablespoons Raspberry Puree
1 cup chopped dark chocolate chucks

Whisk egg yolks and sugar in large bowl until blended. Bring milk and whipping cream to boil in heavy large saucepan over medium heat. Gradually whisk into yolk mixture. Return mixture to saucepan; stir over medium-low heat until custard thickens, about 15 minutes (do not boil). Strain custard into bowl. Cool. Stir port and Raspberry Puree into custard. Refrigerate until cold.

Remove from refrigerator and add dark chocolate chunks. Transfer custard to ice cream maker and process according to manufacturer's instructions. Freeze ice cream in covered container until firm, about 4 hours.

Chef Notes
Can be prepared 3 days ahead.

Port Ice Cream! This recipe also needs a little something. For me, it keeps on turning out a little icy because its not freezing all the way. I originally had frouncesen raspberries in the recipe, but substituted them for the raspberry puree. The whole raspberries were a little too much and the recipe asked for a subtle raspberry presence. The dark chocolate chunks are a must! Enjoy!

Aunt Evelyn's Cantaloupe Sorbet
From the Kitchen of Evelyn Meyer

Makes 12 Servings
2 cups cantaloupe chunks
1 cup white sugar
1/4 cup fresh lemon juice
zest of 1 orange
2-1/4 cups mango juice
1/4 cup Meyer Family Port
3 tablespoons grenadine

Place first four ingredients into blender and blend until smooth. Add mango juice and port. Place into bowl and refrigerate for about an hour.

Pour into the ice cream maker and follow the manufacturer's instructions for freezing. Place in freezer storage container and place in freezer for 4 hours before serving.

 ## Port Poached Pears

Makes 6 Servings
750 ml (1-1/2 bottles) of Meyer
Family Port
1 cup water
1 cup sugar
4 whole cloves
4 (2 x 1 inch) lemon peel strips
1 vanilla bean, split lengthwise
6 firm ripe pears, peeled

Vanilla ice cream

Combine first 5 ingredients in heavy large saucepan. Scrape in seeds from vanilla bean; add bean. Bring to boil, stirring to dissolve sugar. Add pears, reduce heat, cover and simmer until pears are tender when pierced with knife, about 20 minutes. Cool pears completely in syrup. Cover; chill in syrup overnight.

Transfer pears to medium bowl. Cover and refrigerate pears. Boil poaching liquid in heavy large saucepan until reduced to 1 cup, about 35 minutes. Mix in remaining 1 tablespoon anisette. Cover and refrigerate liquid until cold, about 4 hours.

Arrange pears on plates. Drizzle poaching liquid over pears.

Optional: Place scoop of ice cream on one side of each plate. Garnish with biscotti cookies.

Stuffed Baked Apples
Inspired by a friend

Makes 4 Servings
4 Gala apples
1 tablespoon fresh lemon juice
1/4 cup finely chopped dried apricots
2 tablespoons dried currants
2 tablespoons chopped pecans, toasted
2 tablespoons (packed) light brown sugar
1/4 teaspoon cinnamon
1/8 teaspoon ground nutmeg
1 tablespoon butter
4 tablespoons Meyer Family Port
1/2 cup organic apple juice
1/2 teaspoon vanilla

Preheat oven to 350°F. Core apples with corer. Stand apples up and make 4 evenly spaced vertical cuts starting from top of each apple and stopping halfway from bottom to keep apple intact. Brush inside of apples with lemon juice and stand apples in a 9-inch ceramic or glass pie plate.

Toss together apricots, currants, pecans, brown sugar, cinnamon, and nutmeg in a bowl. Rub softened butter into dried-fruit mixture with your fingers until combined well, then pack center of each apple with mixture. Pour a tablespoon of port down the center of each apple. Put a piece of remaining butter on top of each apple. Pour cider and vanilla around apples and cover pie plate tightly with foil.

Bake in middle of oven, basting once, until apples are just tender when pierced with a fork, about 40 minutes. Remove foil and continue to bake until apples are very tender but not falling apart, 20 to 30 minutes more.

Transfer to serving dishes and spoon sauce over and around apples.

Plum Port Tart
Inspired by a friend

Makes 6 servings
Pie Crust
1-1/2 cups all purpose flour
2 tablespoons sugar
1/2 cup butter
3 tablespoons ice water (or additional)

Filling
2 cups Meyer Family Port
1/2 cup packed golden brown sugar, plus 1 tablespoon
1/4 teaspoon cinnamon
1/4 teaspoon nutmeg
1-1/2 pounds plums (5 to 6 medium) pitted and sliced
1 tablespoon all purpose flour

Ginger ice cream

Combine flour and sugar in medium mixing bowl. Cut in butter with pastry knife or fork until mixed in and lumpy consistency. Add in ice water a tablespoon at a time and mix together completely with hands in between adding more water and continue until dough forms. If too dry, add more water, if too sticky add more flour. Form into ball, wrap in plastic wrap and place in refrigerator and let cool for 1 hour. Roll out dough on floured surface and place onto tart pan and do not cut off remaining dough.

Preheat oven to 350°F. Boil Port, 1/2 cup brown sugar, and allspice in large skillet until reduced to 2/3 cup, about 10 minutes. Place plums in large bowl. Sprinkle flour over; toss to coat. Drizzle 1/3 cup syrup over plums; toss to coat. Save remaining syrup.

Place plums into center of crust, drizzle any remaining syrup from bowl over plums. Fold crust edges over plums. Brush crust with water; sprinkle crust and plums with remaining 1 tablespoon brown sugar.

Bake tart until crust is golden and syrup is bubbling, about 1 hour.

Optional: Serve with scoop of ginger ice cream, drizzling additional syrup over.

Apple Raisin Bread Pudding

Makes 8-12 servings
2 cups whole milk
1 cup whipping cream
1 cup sugar
4 large eggs
1 cup Meyer Family Port
1/2 teaspoon ground cinnamon
1/8 teaspoon salt
1 loaf french bread, cut into
3/4-inch cubes
3 large Fuji apple, peeled, cored,
cut into 1/2-inch cubes
1 cup raisins
6 tablespoons of butter
Additional ground cinnamon

Vanilla Ice Cream

Preheat oven to 350°F. Butter 11x7-inch glass baking dish. Whisk first 7 ingredients in large bowl to blend. Fold in bread, apple, and raisins. Pour batter into prepared dish. Slice butter thinly and distribute evenly over the top of the pudding and sprinkle with additional cinnamon. Bake pudding until top is golden brown and center is set, about 1 hour and 15 minutes. Spoon pudding into bowls and serve.

Optional: Serve with vanilla ice cream.

Strawberry Shortcake
Inspired by a friend

Makes 8 Servings
3 cups of sliced strawberries
1/4 cup sugar
1 tablespoon of lemon juice
1/2 cup Meyer Family Port
2 cups whipping cream
4 tablespoons of confectioner's sugar
Vanilla extract
Pound Cake

In mixing bowl, combine sliced strawberries sugar, lemon juice and port and stir. Cover and chill strawberries.

Chill medium mixing bowl and whisk in freezer for 10 minutes. Add cream to medium mixing bowl and blend with whisk or mixer until it begins to foam and thicken. Add sugar and continue to whisk until soft peaks form. Do not over-whip.

Slice pound cake and place on serving dishes. Evenly distribute sliced strawberries over sliced pound cake. Top strawberries and pound cake with a dollop of whipped cream and serve.

Makes 8-9 Servings
Rhubarb
24 ounces fresh rhubarb, trimmed
and cut into 1/2-inch pieces
2/3 cup sugar
1/3 cup Meyer Family Port
2 tablespoons all purpose flour
1 tablespoon unsalted butter,
melted
1/2 teaspoon ground cinnamon

Streusel
3/4 cup all purpose flour
1/2 cup sugar
2 tablespoon finely chopped
crystallized ginger
1 teaspoon finely grated orange
peel
1/4 teaspoon salt
6 tablespoons chilled unsalted
butter, cut into 1/4-inch cubes
1 tablespoon whole milk
1 cup sliced almonds

Vanilla Ice Cream

Preheat oven to 375°F. Combine all of the "Rhubarb" ingredients in large bowl. Place in 8"x 8" pan. Bake for 10 minutes.

Blend flour, sugar, crystallized ginger, orange peel, and salt in processor. Add butter; using on/off turns, blend until coarse crumbs form. Blend in milk (mixture will resemble moist course crumbs). Transfer to medium bowl and stir in almonds. (can prepare and chill 1 day ahead) Crumble streusel over rhubarb, dividing equally. Bake until rhubarb is bubbling and streusel is golden brown, about 20 minutes. Serve crisp warm.

Optional: Add scoop of vanilla ice cream.

Candi's Raspberry Crème Brûlée
From the Kitchen of Candice Buckett

Makes 6 Servings
2-1/2 cups raspberries
1/4 cup Meyer Family Port, plus 3 tablespoons
6 large egg yolks
7 tablespoons sugar
2-1/4 cups whipping cream

3 tablespoons (packed) golden brown sugar

Preheat oven to 325°F. Place raspberries in a bowl and add 1/4 cup port and let sit to soak up port for 15 minutes. Reserve 1/2 cup of the raspberries for garnish. Divide the remaining berries among six standard-size flan dishes.

Whisk yolks and sugar in medium bowl until thick and pale yellow, about 2 minutes. Bring cream to simmer in heavy small saucepan. Gradually whisk hot cream into yolk mixture.

Whisk in port. Divide and pour over berries among the flan dishes. Arrange cups in 13x9x2-inch metal pan. Pour enough hot water into pan to come halfway up sides of cups. Bake custards until gently set in center, about 25 minutes. Remove cups from water and refrigerate uncovered until cold, at least 3 hours. (Can be made 1 day ahead. Cover and keep chilled.)

Preheat broiler. Place custards on baking sheet. Sprinkle 1/2 tablespoon brown sugar onto each. Broil until sugar starts to bubble and color, turning sheet often to prevent burning, about 2 minutes. Chill until topping is hard and brittle, at least 1 hour and up to 6 hours.

Meanwhile, toss berries, brown sugar, and port, if desired, in large bowl. Spoon berry mixture atop custards and serve immediately.

{X} Complimenting Port

Seared Foie Gras with Cranberries and Rhubarb
Mama's Persimmon Pudding
Ruggero's Biscotti
Paula's Chocolate Almond Biscotti Paradiso
Paula's Chocolate Walnut Biscotti Connio
Meyer Lemon Ice Cream
Ginger Ice Cream

Holly's Seared Foie Gras with Cranberries and Rhubarb
From the Kitchen of Chef Holly Peterson, Author of Food and Wine Dynamics

Makes 12 Servings
1 pound Fresh "A" Foie Gras
(try Sonoma Foie Gras; organic, humane & delicious)
2 stalks of rhubarb
2 cups fresh cranberries
zest of one tangerine (finely sliced in a chiffronade)
1/2 cup superfine sugar
Sea Star Fleur de Sel
fresh ground black pepper
fresh Mint
brioche

* It is fine to prepare most of it the day ahead of time, and just finish the dish "a la minute" when you serve it.

Slice the fresh foie gras in 1/3" slices. Place on wax paper on a sheet tray, and refrigerate.

Peel the rhubarb and slice in one inch pieces. Place rhubarb and cranberries in a sauce pan and cover with the superfine sugar and a dash of water. Slowly simmer for 20 minutes, and turn off the heat. As it cools add a finely sliced zest from a tangerine. Finely slice it and add it to the cranberry rhubarb mixture. Refrigerate for at least an hour.

Just before serving heat a sauté pan until hot. Season the foie gras with fleur de sel, and fresh pepper and place directly in the hot pan to sear. Sear about 30 seconds on each side or until golden. Be careful not to over cook or you will melt away all of your delicious foie gras. With a flat slotted spatula, remove the foie gras and place on a kitchen towel to absorb the excess fat.

Heat the plates that you will serve this on.
Place a little of cranberry rhubarb sauce on each plate and top with foie gras.

Garnish with a mint leaf and a basket of sliced, toasted brioche.
Now have a glass of Meyer Family Port and savor this first course. It is a great way to celebrate something special!

Mama's Persimmon Pudding
From the Kitchen of Bonny Meyer

Makes 12 Servings
1-1/2 cup Sugar
1-1/2 cup Flour
1-1/2 teaspoon ground cinnamon
1/2 teaspoon ground nutmeg
1 tablespoon baking soda
Water
1-1/2 cup ripe persimmon pulp
2 eggs
1-1/2 cup chopped pitted prunes
1 cup coarsely chopped almonds,
walnuts, or hazelnuts
3/4 cup brandy, plus more to pour over
2 teaspoon vanilla
1-1/2 teaspoon lemon juice
3/4 cup Butter melted and cooled to
lukewarm

Mix sugar, flour, cinnamon and nutmeg. In a bowl, stir soda with 3 tablespoon hot water, then mix in persimmon pulp and eggs; beat until blended. Add sugar mixture, prunes, nuts 1/3 cup brandy, vanilla, lemon juice and butter. Stir until mixed.

Pour batter into a buttered 9-10 cups pudding mold. Place on a rack in a deep pan. Add 1 inch water, cover pan and steam over medium heat until pudding in firm when lightly pressed in the center, about 2-1/2 hours. Add boiling water as needed.

Uncover pudding and let stand on a rack to cool slightly, about 15 min. Invert onto a dish, lift off mold and serve. If desired, make ahead of time, cover with cheesecloth and moisten evenly with brandy. Wrap in foil.

> *"A wonderful winter Holiday treat. It is customary to only moisten the pudding with brandy once... Although it has been known to happen more than once, and can be dangerous!"*
>
> - Bonny Meyer

"Buon Appetito!"
- Ruggero Gigli

Ruggero's Biscotti
From the Kitchen of Chef Ruggero Gigli

Makes 120 Cookies

5 cups flour, plus 1 cup
3 cups granulated sugar
2 teaspoons baking soda
Pinch of salt
6 eggs
2 egg yolks
1 teaspoon vanilla extract
1 teaspoon almond extract
1 teaspoon orange extract
1 teaspoon lemon extract
1 orange, grate peel and juice
2 lemons, grate peel and juice
3-1/2 cups toasted, coarsely chopped almonds
1/2 cup pine nuts
12 ounces dried figs, stems discarded and chopped

Preheat the oven to 375°F. Oil (4) 14-inch pizza pans (or large cookie sheets) with olive oil. Distribute and wipe off excess oil with clean paper towel. Dust oiled sheets with flour. Mix together 5 cups flour, sugar, baking soda and salt and heap on counter. Make a crater in the flour mixture (like when making pasta).

In small mixing bowl, beat and combine eggs, yolks, extracts, orange peel and juice and lemon peel and juice. Pour ingredients into the crater of the flour mixture. With hands, slowly incorporate dry mixture into liquid mixture, working from the center outward. Use additional 1 cup of flour to sprinkle over the counter to prevent the dough from sticking. Work dough until well blended. Slowly add nuts and figs. Knead 15 minutes. Divide dough into 4 parts and roll into balls. Divide each ball into thirds and roll into long sticks, 2-inches in diameter, in lengths to fit the baking sheets. Place (3) rolls on each pan

Place (2) of the sheets in oven and bake for 15 minutes. Remove first batch from the oven and place second batch, other (2) baking sheets, in the oven for 15 minutes. After baking both batches, reduce oven temperature to 300°F. Slide rolls onto counter with spatula. Cut diagonally in 1/2 – inch slices. Arrange with cut side up on the pans and place back into oven for an additional 10 minutes.

Paula's Chocolate Almond Biscotti Paradiso
From the Kitchen of Paula Rae Menna

Makes About 40 Cookies
1/2 cup butter
3/4 cup of sugar
2 eggs
1 teaspoon real almond extract,
plus 1 teaspoon
2 cups flour
1-1/2 teaspoon baking powder
1/4 teaspoon salt
3 squares of chopped semisweet
chocolate
1 cup chopped toasted almonds
1 cup semisweet chocolate chips

Beat butter and sugar until light and fluffy. Beat in eggs and almond extract. Mix in flour, baking powder and salt. Stir in chocolate and almonds

Shape dough into 2 logs (14" X 1 ½"). Place 2" apart on greased and floured baking sheet.

Bake 25 minutes at 325°F. Let cool for 5 minutes. Cut logs into ¾" sliced and place back into the oven for 10 minutes or until slightly dry. Let stand and cool.

Melt 1 cup chocolate chips in a double boiler. Add in 1 teaspoon of almond extract to the melted chocolate. Spread a very thin layer on to the cooled biscotti.

Paula's Chocolate Walnut Biscotti Connio
From the Kitchen of Paula Rae Menna

Makes About 40 Cookies
1/2 cup butter
3/4 cup of sugar
2 eggs
1 teaspoon real vanilla extract
2 cups flour
1-1/2 teaspoon baking powder
1/4 teaspoon salt
4 squares of chopped semisweet chocolate
1 cup chopped toasted walnuts

Beat butter and sugar until light and fluffy. Beat in eggs and vanilla extract. Mix in flour, baking powder and salt. Stir in chocolate and walnuts.

Shape dough into 2 logs (14" X 1 ½"). Place 2" apart on greased and floured baking sheet.

Bake 25 minutes at 325°F.. Let cool for 5 minutes. Cut logs into ¾" sliced and place back into the oven for 10 minutes or until slightly dry. Let stand and cool.

Meyer Lemon Ice Cream

Makes about 1 quart
1 teaspoon grated Meyer lemon zest
1/4 cup fresh Meyer lemon juice
1 cup sugar
2 eggs
1-1/2 cup whipping cream
1 cup whole milk
1 dash salt

Combine ingredients in a blender container or food processor and process until smooth. Cover and refrigerate until ready to freeze. Pour into the ice cream maker and follow the manufacturer's instructions for freezing. Place in freezer storage container and place in freezer for 4 hours before serving.

Ginger Ice Cream

Makes 1 quart
4 large egg yolks
1/2 cup sugar
1/4 cup coarsely grated peeled
fresh ginger root
2 tablespoons water
1 cup whole milk
2 cup heavy cream
1 teaspoon vanilla
1/2 cup crystallized ginger

In a large bowl lightly whisk yolks. In a large saucepan cook sugar, fresh ginger root, and water over moderate heat, stirring occasionally, about 5 minutes. Add milk and cream and bring to a simmer. Add hot milk mixture to yolks in a slow stream, whisking, and pour into pan. Cook custard over moderately low heat, stirring constantly, until a thermometer registers 170°F. (Do not let boil.)

Pour custard through a fine sieve into cleaned bowl and stir in vanilla. Cool custard. Chill custard, its surface covered with plastic wrap, until cold, at least 3 hours and up to 1 day.

Finely chop crystallized ginger. Freeze custard in an ice-cream maker, adding crystallized ginger three quarters of way through freezing process. Transfer ice cream to an airtight container and put in freezer to harden. Ice cream may be made 1 week ahead.

Sources

"Meyer Family Port, the fortified zinfandel made by Matt and Karen Meyer at their winery in Mendocino County, occupies a unique position on the surprisingly long list of sweet wines produced in California. Most of these wines are made for tasting room crowds or mailing lists, or otherwise fall into the "afterthought dessert wine" category. The Meyer's Port, on the other hand, is an unfailing show-stopper."

- Tony Poer, Meyer Family Port Sales Manager

Get Meyer Family Port direct from Meyer Family Cellars. Also, find a list of local distributors and stores on the Meyer Family Cellars website.

Meyer Family Cellars

Meyer Family Cellars
P.O. Box 294
Yorkville, CA 95494
{Tel} 707.895.2341
{Fax} 707.895.2817
{e-mail} info@mfcellars.com

Seasonal Suggestions

For the best results, use the ingredients while they are in season! Don't be buying strawberries in the winter that are shipped from Peru. Notice that the *(**starred**) recipes may only be available during those particular seasons, because they don't grow figs and persimmons in Peru during the Spring.

Autumn Seasonal Dishes
Apple Raisin Bread Pudding, 130
*Baked Figs, 67
*Cin's Cranberry Sauce with Port
  & Dried Fruit, 60
*Fig and Goat Cheese Crostini, 68
Grilled Pears with Blackberry Port Sauce, 86
Gruyere, Prosciutto and Pear
  Pizza with Spring Greens, 100
Holly's Seared Foie Gras with Cranberries
  and Rhubarb, 138
*Jerry's Figs with Crème Fraiche, 48
*Pat's Pumpkin Marble Salad, 97
Pear and Pecan Salad with Port Vinaigrette, 94
Plum Port Tart, 129
Poached Pears, 125
Rhubarb Port Crisp, 134
Ruggero's Filetto con Fichi, 108
Stuffed Baked Apples, 126

Winter Seasonal Dishes
Baked Oysters, 77
Braised Short Ribs, 107
Glühwein, 24
*Mama's Persimmon Pudding, 139
*Meyer Lemon Ice Cream, 142
Tatu's Spiced Port Cookies, 120

Spring Seasonal Dishes
*Sliced Strawberries in Port, 45
*Strawberry Shortcake, 133

Summer Seasonal Dishes
Aunt Evelyn's Cantaloupe Sorbet, 123
Drunken Cantaloupe, 46
*Grilled Peaches with Sweet Port Sauce, 89
Kels' Tomato and Goat Cheese Flatbread, 74
Lala's Grilled Tomatoes, 90
Port Raspberry Lemonade, 23
Port Tomato Sauce, 62
Sangria, 21

Port Menus

Sunday Brunch
Spring Fresh
Summer Barbecue
'After a Late Night' Breakfast
Autumn Dinner
Winter Feast
Winter Vegetarian Dinner
Casual Weekend Dinner Party
Lunch in the Garden
Cocktail Party
Casual Dinner In
Dining Italiano Presto

Sunday Brunch
Rosy Cheek Fizz
Port Caramelized Bacon
Desi's Drunken Raspberry Crumb Cake
Mushroom and Gruyere Bread Pudding
Tipsy Fruit Salad

Spring Fresh
Sangria
Portobello and Tomato Bruschetta
Pear & Pecan Salad with Port Vinaigrette
Strawberry Shortcake

Summer Barbecue
Port Raspberry Lemonade
Grilled Asparagus
Lala's Grilled Tomatoes
Ribs with Port Barbecue Sauce or Chocolate Barbecue Sauce
Grilled Peaches with Sweet Port Sauce

Autumn Dinner
Asparagus & Prosciutto
Mama Meyer's Mushrooms
Roast Beef Tenderlion with Port Sauce
Poached Pears with Vanilla Ice Cream

Winter Feast
Glühwein
Baked Oysters
Onions with Currant, Port and Balsamic Glaze
Mixed Greens with Port Balsamic Vinaigrette
Braised Short Ribs
Rhubarb Port Crisp

Casual Dinner In
Mixed Greens with Port Balsamic Vinaigrette
Captain Fantastic's Swedish Meatballs
Candi's Chocolate Chip Cookies and Port Drizzle

'After a Late Night' Breakfast
Port Chantilly
Sliced Strawberries in Port
Candied Pecans
Portified Waffles & Pancakes or Port French Toast

Winter Vegetarian Dinner
Pat's Pumpkin Marble Soup
Norma's Beet, Cherry and Port Risotto
Mama's Persimmon Pudding

Casual Weekend Dinner Party
Kels' Tomato and Goat Cheese Flatbread
Mixed Greens with Port Balsamic Vinaigrette
Rosemary Burgers with Port Balsamic Glaze
Apple Raisin Bread Pudding

Lunch in the Garden
Drunken Cantaloupe
Gruyère, Prosciutto and Pear Pizza with Spring Greens
Grilled Asparagus
Port Ice Cream with Chocolate Chunks topped with Raspberries in Port

Cocktail Party
Baked Figs
Roasted Portobello Crostini
Seared Foie Gras with Cranberries and Rhubarb
Sliced Crostini
Lala's Meatball Appetizer
Meyer family Port Chocolate Truffles

Dining Italiano Alfresco
Fig and Goat Cheese Crostini
Pasta with Port Tomato Sauce
Ruggero's Filetto con Fichi
Biscotti

Port Index

Table of Equivalents

The exact equivalents in the following tables have been rounded for convenience.

Liquid Measures

U.S.	Metric
1/4 teaspoon	1.25 milliliters
1/2 teaspoon	2.5 milliliters
1 teaspoon	5 milliliters
1 tablespoon (3 teaspoons)	15 milliliters
1 fluid ounce (ounces, 2 tablespoons)	30 milliliters
	60 milliliters
1/4 cup	80 milliliters
1/3 cup	120 milliliters
1/2 cup	240 milliliters
1 cup	480 milliliters
1 pint (2 cups)	960 milliliters
1 quart (4 cups, 32 ounces)	3.84 liters
1 gallon (4 quarts)	
	28 grams
1 ounce (ounces, by weight)	454 grams
1 pound (pound)	1 kilogram
2.2 pounds (pounds)	

Oven Temperature

Fahrenheit	Celsius	Gas
250	120	1/2
275	140	1
300	150	2
325	160	3
350	180	4
375	190	5
400	200	6
425	220	7
450	230	8
475	240	9
500	260	10

Length

U.S.	Metric
	3 millimeters
1/8 inch	6 millimeters
1/4 inch	12 millimeters
1/2 inch	2.5 centimeters
1 inch	

Photo: Lisa Batto

Holly Meyer

brings years of experience in the wine industry and a great interest in the culinary arts. Along with her passion for food and wine, Holly also has her BA in Art History and a Masters in Architecture. She lives in the Bay Area and practices sustainable architecture in the Napa Valley. This is her first book.